The
Elegant
Table

THE ELEGANT TABLE

By Barbara Wirth

Photographs by Pascal Hinous

Preface by James de Coquet

Harry N. Abrams, Inc., Publishers, New York

Translated from the French by Danielle Lawrence de Froidmont

English-language edition:
Project Manager: Leta Bostelman
Editor: Alexandra Bonfante-Warren
Typographic design: Carol Robson

Library of Congress Cataloging-in-Publication Data

Wirth, Barbara.
The elegant table / by Barbara Wirth; photographs by Pascal
Hinous; foreword, James de Coquet.
p.   cm.
ISBN 0-8109-0892-1
1. Table setting and decoration.   2. Entertaining—France.
3. Upper classes—France—Social life and customs.   I. Hinous,
Pascal.   II. Title.
TX879.W53 1988
642'.8—dc19   88-10501

Copyright © 1987 Editions Presse Audiovisuel E.P.A.
English translation copyright © 1988 Harry N. Abrams, Inc.

Published in 1988 by Harry N. Abrams, Incorporated, New York
All rights reserved. No part of the contents of this book may be
reproduced without the written permission of the publisher

A Times Mirror Company

Printed in Belgium
Bound in France

Contents

The afternoon

Soliloquies and tête-à-têtes

Dinner

Grand soirées

Later . . .

Double Duty

Details

MADAME IS SERVED

by James de Coquet

The art of the table begins at breakfast. The components of this meal must be arranged on their tray with military precision. The most advanced element — the teapot — is placed in the right-hand corner, for it will be the first to come into play.

With regard to the teapot, follow the English rule: "Always bring the teapot to the kettle, not the kettle to the teapot." This ensures that the water is poured onto the tea as soon as it starts to boil, when it stops whistling.

To the left of the teapot go the cup, the butter dish, and the sugar bowl. Behind this advance echelon, in the left-hand corner, comes the milk, which brings us to a further observation: it is commonly believed to be "very British" to pour the milk into the cup before the tea. In fact, while all the old housekeepers in London and many secretaries in the City do so, neither Mrs. Thatcher nor Princess Diana subscribes to this method.

The edible elements of the meal are arranged from left to right and depend on one's individual preference. Slices of toast should neither be piled on top of each other nor wrapped in a napkin, which will make them go soft. Instead, they must be placed vertically in a rack — which need not be silver. Orange marmalade and, if desired, black cherry jam are served in small bowls.

What should a tea set be made of? Preferably, Minton or Chantilly china. Drinking café au lait is no crime — as long as it is drunk from a large faience cup from Gien, for example. In this case, the orange marmalade will be replaced by apricot jam, which becomes café au lait as mourning does Electra.

A daily paper is the correct complement to breakfast; the *Figaro* in France, a London or New York *Times* across the Channel or the Atlantic. A good weather forecast is also an excellent addition.

Should the table determine the décor of the dining room, or vice versa? This is an insoluble problem. It is all too easy to imagine falling in love with twenty-four rare plates and a decorative centerpiece, and therefore having to totally change one's surroundings. On the other hand, a sixteenth-century gentleman settling in the Marais or in the Quai Conti quarter could just send his servant to the sale room and buy a new dinner set.

A well-known Parisian lady, in the twilight of her life, withdrew to Cannes. The proud owner of dinner services that were unique in France and probably in the world, she could serve forty people lunch on Sèvres "cabbage-leaf," and her blue and white "Canton" rested, on occasion, on flat vermilion place plates. She also owned a magnificent "Capo di Monte" set, the best, from the period of Charles III. (In those days, a king of Naples or of the Two Sicilies could be fired like the manager of a failing company today. The deposed Charles III went off to Spain to retrain, taking with him his china manufacturers and their source of inspiration, a man called Gricci. This is why the Ferdinand IV "Capo di Monte" is much less prized by connoisseurs than the Charles III version. However, should you be offered one or two pieces of the former, do not refuse them.)

The history of the ceramic arts is a love story, full of quarrels, separations, and betrayals. In Naples, they said their last farewells. In France, they were unfaithful. A group of workers at a hard-paste porcelain factory in Sèvres left, to found a factory in Vincennes for soft-paste porcelain, which had just been invented. They immediately found a patron in Madame de Pompadour, who herself resembled a Dresden figurine. Feeling that Vincennes was too far from Versailles, she persuaded the manufacturers to return to the village of Sèvres, where they were installed in Lully's former summer residence. Apart from Madame de Pompadour, the list of customers of the period included

Fragonard and the Colombe sisters from the Opéra, who built a delightful "folly" at Soisy-sous-Forêt that is still intact. A royal favorite, a painter of courtship scenes, two Opéra beauties—how wonderful to think that soft-paste porcelain first appeared in a world ruled by love!

Since then, many plates have been broken, but love survives. Heads of households of both sexes are very protective of their table settings. For them, the washing-machine is a modern-day Attila. The smallest scratch on the rim of a plate is an irreversible wound that causes them physical anguish.

The era of soft-paste porcelain was followed by the Revolution and the Reign of Terror. There was no more entertaining. The aristocrats survived by setting up tables in front of their *hôtels* and serving "everlasting soup" to the sansculottes and the common people. Plates changed in style to reflect the times. These Revolutionary plates are very expensive today—but Dr. Guillotine's "national razor" also cuts the appetite.

We must not be hypnotized by the past. Even if you own a set of diabolo-shaped glasses dating from before the invention of crystalware, your guests will prefer to drink your Médoc or Sauterne from Baccarat made the day before yesterday.

As for plates and dishes, today's Limoges porcelain, its clay still mined from the famous Saint-Yrieux deposit, is just as fine as that used by Turgot, while at Riez, near Moustiers, a great artist named Simonne Favier has rediscovered the secret of Clérissy. Her services, with twisted rims and hand-painted nightshade designs, rival their predecessors.

A table reflects the mood of the moment. One evening, you may gather your friends around a tablecloth made from a printed calico bedspread, the next, around flowered organdy over pink satin padded with felt.

Remember that the wonderful tables you will see in this book are not immutable, like Manet's *Déjeuner sur l'herbe*. They can be constantly varied. After all, tables are only states of mind.

JACQUES GRANGE

Brunch under Colette's skylight

So sensitive is Jacques Grange to the beauty of a place that he responds instantly to its soul and its past. It was, therefore, not chance, but a kind of imperative that drew him to Colette's onetime apartment at the Palais-Royal. This imperative appears all the more irresistible if one is aware that this interior designer's favorite period is the turn of the twentieth century. Atmosphere and mélange are the keywords for this setting in muted tones, in which a table is laid for brunch. The mahogany chairs and remarkable folding console table are English and date from 1910; the Boukhara table cover is Turkish; the nineteenth-century screens, of ebony and brass, are Russian; and the chandelier was made in 1910 by Serrurier-Bovy. The table setting is an equally free composition: Gien plates from 1900 with the arms of Diane of Poitiers and Henry II, Primavera cups from 1930, a nineteenth-century English boxwood egg-holder, and embroidered napkins from Marrakesh. This is a subtle, allusive universe, to which a picture and a mirror provide the twofold key: Louise Abbema's *Intérieur avec objets de Sarah Bernhardt* illustrates Jacques Grange's love of the theater, while the convex mirror, reflecting a distorted image of the whole room, hints at his fascination with the interplay of perspectives and optical illusions.

THE BARONNE GÉRARD DE WALDNER

At break of day

The morning paper brought in with the breakfast tray is tied with a pink satin ribbon. Presented so prettily, the news can only be good! But this charming touch is just one instance of the perfect good taste that pervades every detail of Sylvia de Waldner's life—witness her bedroom and her breakfast. The organdy tray cloth and lawn napkins are both embroidered with the same monogram as the sheets, in one of the shades of blue of the chintz canopy. (Sylvia de Waldner loves linens, preferring those she finds in Florence.) She drinks her tea from an English porcelain tea set decorated with violets. A small bouquet of miniature roses in a silver cup brings an additional note of freshness to this moment of calm before a long day.

THE COMTESSE JEAN D'ORMESSON

Christmas morning

On Christmas day, Françoise d'Ormesson gives her family a delicious surprise. With her customary discreet sophistication, she prepares an enchanting breakfast, a model of elegance and simplicity. The table, covered with a paper cloth, is set up beside the fireplace in the morning room. It is a symphony of reds, greens, and white, in the best Christmas tradition: a large bouquet of freesias, red roses, and branches of viburnum; nineteenth-century Minton cups; English silverware; and a nineteenth-century French orangeade jug. A subtle play of paper and silver, the ephemeral and the enduring; the mood of a day, on the one hand, on the other, tradition. The blazing fire and the presents wrapped in shiny paper with large satin bows contribute to the success of this charming scene—a delightful improvisation on the lively theme of a Christmas morning.

THE CONTESSA BRANDOLINI D'ADDA

A pink breakfast

Teas, potpourris, literature, antiques . . . to blend these requires more than savoir-faire, for it is an art form, and the Contessa Brandolini d'Adda's favorite mode of expression. Using her love of the color pink as a theme, she gathers objects and pieces of furniture from all periods and countries. Her breakfast, served in the kitchen–dining room designed by Mongiardino, is a masterpiece of gentle harmony: English Gothic chairs, pink porcelain, a Tiffany coffeepot, Venetian glasses in Russian glass-holders, nineteenth-century French Klotz plates, all on an English marble marquetry table. Here, there is no hierarchy; the Contessa Brandolini d'Adda has compiled this collection a piece at a time, governed only by her own taste. The result is an exquisite . . . "object lesson."

More than 400 Abrams titles are currently available at your local bookseller.

PHILIPPE VENET

By the water's edge

On one side, a stretch of water is glimpsed through the hedge; on the other side is the swimming pool. Philippe Venet enjoys the poetic calm of the one and the relaxation afforded by the other, and so, on weekends, he likes having his lunch between the two. Everything here is natural and well-balanced. All is straw, wood, and the colors of nature—leaf-green and sunlight-yellow—and each object seems echoed in the world of the garden: straw mats; yellow marbled plates; yellow-rimmed glasses from Venice; gilded bronze, bamboo-pattern cutlery; and green linen napkins. Philippe Venet made up the bouquet that very morning from his own roses: Iceberg, Mme Meilland, Marrakesh, and Champagne. Here, lunch is a kind of interlude, a bridge perfectly poised between two waters.

FRANÇOIS CATROUX

Table with camellias

For this intimate lunch, François Catroux has had the table set amid the masculine elegance of the neoclassical library. The dominant element—mahogany—is brightened by pale pink camellias from the garden, arranged in silver cups. François Catroux, who makes many trans-Atlantic trips, went to Bloomingdale's for the large Japanese dish and plates, which are simply placed on blue and white linen "Willow Pattern" mats. The mahogany of the library, tables, and Demay "Retour d'Égypte" chairs; the lacquer of the Coromandel screens; and the marble of the fireplace together create a harmonious whole. On the floor, a masterly balance of past and present: the pattern of the carpet is a cozy interpretation of the traditional tiling in eighteenth-century homes. In such a room, earthly and spiritual sustenance are certain to complement each other agreeably.

JEAN SCHLUMBERGER

The intimacy of objects

Who could go to Tiffany's and take the elevator to Jean Schlumberger's domain without a feeling of tremendous excitement? So many marvelous ingenuities have been devised here, at the hands of this magician. So many wonders— boxes and jewels—have been forged here by this unique artist, who has combined gold and precious or semiprecious stones as no one before him dared. In the apartment in which Jean Schlumberger lives today, and which he calls his "attic," the dining room is all white, with large white curtains breaking at the floor. The room is an unpretentious jewel-case for an enchanting table. Indeed, it is difficult to know what pleases most: the gilded bronze African-head bells from the early nineteenth century; the collection of silver animal-head saltcellars; the Sheffield white-porcelain cutlery designed by Syrie Maugham; or the porcelain cigarette case with its trompe l'oeil malachite decoration. Then, like rests in a musical score, Jean Schlumberger's own boxes. At the mere sight of them, one imagines a thousand reasons—cigarettes, pills, cuff links, or pins—why one would need them. The batik tablecloth, the nineteenth-century Chinese plates with their crab decoration, the etched Vieux Baccarat tumblers, all compose a setting that is closely akin to Johnny Schlumberger's art: a self-portrait–table in his own inimitable style.

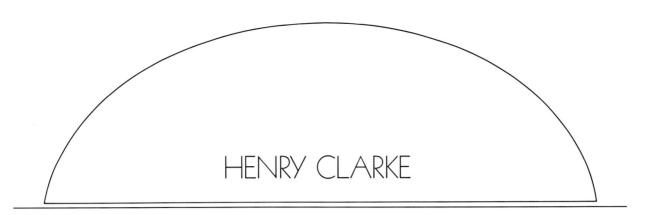

HENRY CLARKE

The art of composition

When you spend all your life with your eye fixed to a lens, as the photographer Henry Clarke does, you acquire such a sense of composition that you instantly perceive an order in any group of objects, any mass in a garden, or any setting at all. Henry Clarke's main concern in his camerawork is to bring out the best in his subject and its surroundings without intruding himself into the proceedings. One finds this same discretion and reserve in this décor for a summer lunch, prepared in the cool, vaulted loggia of his attractive home. Once the residence of the brotherhood of the Pénitents Noirs, the house opens onto four asymmetrical levels with loggias everywhere looking out over both the rock of Monaco and a marvelous garden of box hedges, lemon trees, orange trees, and jasmine shrubs. The table, surrounded by Provençal Louis XVI chairs, has a Portuguese damask bedspread as a tablecloth. There are Nevers plates and Biot glasses, a silver pepperpot dating from 1900, and Sheffield stainless-steel and white porcelain cutlery designed by Syrie Maugham. In the center of the table, a Mexican pyramid displays seashells gathered by the master of the house, who has collected some of the world's rarest specimens. Lunching here, you would be more likely to conjure up a sublime model straight out of Henry Clarke's latest book of photos, than the ghost of a Pénitent Noir.

THE DUC
AND
DUCHESSE DE MOUCHY

Lunch at Haut-Brion

It cannot be confirmed that Talleyrand lived at Haut-Brion, but one thing is certain: his diplomatic skills were aptly supported by the quality of his wine! Today, the Duc and Duchesse de Mouchy preside over this first-class Graves and Médoc vineyard. Continuing the work of her family, the Dillons, the Duchesse de Mouchy has spared no effort to re-create Haut-Brion's original character. The estate is intensely active, and there are usually many guests at lunch. This is served at small tables for six to eight, arranged around a buffet table, on which an eighteenth-century Bacchus from Bordeaux is enthroned and bears the inscription "Haut-Brion." The tablecloths are printed calico, the Wedgwood plates date from the 1930s, and the glasses are etched with the Haut-Brion monogram. From Talleyrand to Douglas Dillon, diplomacy has been the order of the day at Haut-Brion, and with their exquisite courtesy, the Duc and Duchesse endow this great tradition with the tasteful simplicity of their elegance.

MADAME JEAN-LOUIS DUMAS

Picnic under the Paris sky

Only grass and box hedge adorn this simple garden aerie; Rena and Jean-Louis Dumas have preferred to leave the starring role for this setting to the ever-changing light of the Parisian sky, and to the monuments that can be seen from here: the Invalides, the Concorde, the Opéra, and many others. Whether it is her desire to share with others her daydreaming on passing clouds or her passion for this breathtaking view, any excuse will do for Rena Dumas to invite friends for a picnic on the terrace, as soon as the weather permits. She entertains *à la japonaise,* on the ground, with canvas mattresses and cushions surrounding a low table covered in green chintz—another lawn, perhaps, which Rena, in her artistic way, likes to decorate with porcelain toucans—a whimsical touch from Hermès. What fun to play at "picnic" with baskets and boxes taken from a wonderful trunk by Keller the goldsmith, with tumblers, porcelain, and silverware. Primroses in silver bowls they found in Madras are a cheerful touch against the green monochrome. After a heavenly picnic, one has only to lie back on the cushions and count sheep in the lingering, nonpareil Parisian sky. . . .

ANNE-MARIE DE GANAY

A floral lunch

Anne-Marie de Ganay is as good a collector of antiques as she is a decorator, and she takes pleasure in arranging her table around her latest finds—always with comfortable, English-style charm. In her dining room, the theme is floral, dominated by the greens and pinks of a pretty primrose-patterned chintz that sets the tone for the table. There are pink and white organdy mats, hand-painted plates with a large floral design, family silver, an eighteenth-century cruet, glass dishes, little pots of helxine, pink and clear glasses, Regency candlesticks, a Gallé pitcher, and— given pride of place at the center of the table—a luxuriant trompe l'oeil cabbage! The mahogany table, white-lacquered chairs, and Ribemont-Dessaignes canvas all play their part in this pleasing ensemble, ideal, for example, for a Sunday lunch before the races.

MONSIEUR AND MADAME GÉRALD VAN DER KEMP

Lunch at Monet's

Here at Giverny, Gérald van der Kemp has erased the ravages of time and neglect so well that one might easily forget the years that have passed and believe oneself invited to lunch by Claude Monet himself. Seeing the house and garden today, it is difficult to imagine the state of abandonment and dilapidation Gérald van der Kemp found them in. Working from remnants of furniture and from Monet's photographs and canvases, Gérald re-created everything, down to the last detail: walls, ceiling, and furniture were repainted the original two shades of yellow; the blue porcelain pieces and the Japanese prints by Hiroshige, Utamaro, and Hokusai are once again where the painter originally placed them. The garden that Monet cared for so deeply — he spoke of it more than he did of his painting — is once again brilliant with contrasting colors. It has inspired Madame van der Kemp's table decoration, which is studded with personal touches, like the red roses from the garden, which grace eighteenth-century bud vases collected by the former curator of Versailles; the American silverware; and the collection of Chinese porcelain cats that Monet would no doubt have appreciated. On a linen tablecloth with openwork border, a gift from Mme Porthault, is laid the painter's blue and yellow dinner service, entirely remade at Limoges from a few surviving pieces. Mirage or re-creation . . . One almost expects to see Marguerite, the cook, appear with Monet's salad, which he always seasoned himself, smothering it with black pepper!

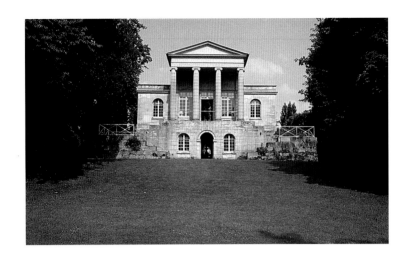

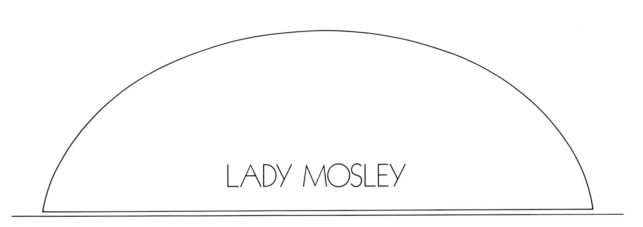

LADY MOSLEY

The best of both worlds

Lady Mosley — *née* Diana Mitford — lives in Orsay in the delightful "Temple of Glory." Built in 1800 by the architect Vignon for General Moreau, who had just won the victory of Hohenlinden, this Palladian-inspired "folly" perches on a hill that slopes down to a lake. The landscape displays a harmonious combination of French-style garden and English-style park, just as Lady Mosley combines the best of both worlds in her life. In the dining room, on a mahogany Empire table overlooked by a bust of Lord Chatham, she has juxtaposed typically English silverware and tablemats, slipware plates, green glass finger bowls, a saltcellar that she believes to be Sèvres, a vermeil pineapple from Augsburg, and fine Directoire chairs from Modena with their original blue and gold paint. A very attractive and . . . European point of view!

CLAUDE AND FRANÇOIS-XAVIER LALANNE

Poetic fantasy in the garden

With affectionate good humor, a sense of poetry tempered with irony, and a gentle disrespect for the functions of objects, Claude Lalanne has improvised a pastoral tête-à-tête in her garden. Since we are in the country, the fauna and flora are invited but they are revised and modified in characteristic Lalanne fashion, while François-Xavier's sheep-chairs survey the scene from afar. On the sculptor's table, two Sèvres plates rescued from friends' dinners emphasize the completely surrealistic silver cutlery— astonishing compositions of leaves, flowers, and insects, which Claude made in 1966 for an exhibition at Alexandre Iolas's. Equally surrealistic are little bronze feet for the salt and pepper and François-Xavier's smallest sheep, the gilded bronze carafe stopper. The bronze chairs that Claude made for the Williamsburg Museum embody a theme of palm trees and nesting birds. What marvelous whimsy in the Lalannes' return to nature, and how well they have shared the task: he produces his strange and wonderful beasts, and she, her mythical fauna and flora!

YVES VIDAL

Easter eggs

Daffodils and eggs are the center of attention when Yves Vidal invites a few close friends for Easter lunch. He creates an intimate mood leavened with charming fantasy: on each guest's plate, a chocolate egg, crowned with a daffodil, encloses a present. Like an offering to spring, a large silver punch bowl, full of still more eggs and daffodils, serves as a centerpiece. Charles Sévigny set the table for Yves Vidal, covering it with a fine old Jacquard cloth, probably from Central Europe. Contrasting with the simplicity of the eggs and flowers is the silver: English plates, boxes, shells, saltshaker, and cutlery. At each place setting are two glasses hand-blown from a Louis XIV model, and both the same size — for those who appreciate water as much as wine. Yves Vidal, who now lives mostly at York Castle in Tangiers, has gathered together in his small Paris flat some of his favorite possessions. He skillfully puts an old principle into practice: the most attractive homes are made, not with new purchases, but from the things one has always loved.

PHILIPPINE DE ROTHSCHILD

The magic of Mouton

To enter the Great Room at Mouton is a unique experience. The visitor is enchanted at once by the loveliness of its rhythmical proportions, by the arched windows, by the contrast between its unadorned quality and the magical aura of the objects within it, and by the beauty of the stone-and-tile floor, inspired by the courtyard of a Mantuan palace. There is no dining room at Mouton; Philippine de Rothschild sets up the lunch table in the Great Room instead, its position depending on the number of guests expected. On the coral-pink tablecloth are remarkable Sèvres-Révolution plates. These are of red, white, and blue porcelain, with scalloped edges, and were made at home by Sèvres factory workers during the French Revolution. Baronne Pauline collected plates, of which she was so fond that she had her "book of services" brought to her every morning so that she could choose—among the Creil et Montereau, the Sarreguemines, or the Vieux Bordeaux—which to use for the cheese and the dessert on that particular day. The silver and vermeil English cutlery dates from the mid-nineteenth century, and is decorated with hunting scenes in relief. The flowers—papyrus, Mme Meilland roses, and cosmos—are arranged in small Japanese pots used as bud vases. The wine is served in a manner unique to Château-Mouton Rothschild. The carafes, custom-made in Venice for Baron Philippe, are placed, not on the dining table, but on Japanese lacquered tables, with handkerchiefs around the necks in memory of a wartime custom: since there was not enough soap to wash the tablecloths, carafes were wrapped in handkerchiefs to avoid staining. The tradition of the handkerchief, which is, naturally, the color of Bordeaux, has continued, for, as the Château-Mouton motto has it, *Mouton suis!*—"I am Mouton!"

THE COMTE AND COMTESSE LOUIS-AMÉDÉE DE MOUSTIER

Shooting break

Hunting at Caulincourt with the Moustiers does not allow for a real sit-down lunch, for the days are too short. Instead, a log fire is built in a forest clearing, where the majordomo, who has arrived in a Land Rover loaded with flasks and large hampers, sets up a table on trestles. The menu is as appropriate as it is unchanging: hot broth; stew; Maroilles, the local cheese; Saint-Quentin *conversations* for dessert; and, of course, a great wine. All served simply in Arcopal dishes. The backdrop is the Château of Caulincourt, erected in 1930 on the ruins of a very old house destroyed in the First World War. It is the work of an exceptional artist, André Beloborodoff, who has created only two or three buildings; an architect, designer, etcher, and decorator, he was also responsible for Caulincourt's interiors. A Palladian palace built in the department of the Aisne by a Russian architect: whether blending such different worlds or improvising a simple open-air lunch, the Moustiers leave their elegant mark on everything they do.

DICK DUMAS

A color merry-go-round

Dick Dumas's house in the south of France has a colorful history. A former inn, it is situated just across from the old medieval village of Oppède-le-Vieux. Dick Dumas often went for walks in this area that he loves, when one day he learnt that the inn was for sale. Today, the house is entirely done in the country look so dear to him. The luncheon table is set in the winter garden in front of large picture windows partially hidden by oleanders. The table is a true symphony of colors; the blue, green, red, and yellow of the Souleiado tablecloth are each echoed by various elements on the table. The yellow plates, bearing a cherry design, are copies of eighteenth-century Aix faience, which the decorator has made locally. The napkins tied around the bottles and artistically crumpled in the large glasses are green, as are the small faience plates from Apt, against which the ox-blood lacquered bowls stand out. Blue, yellow, and green are repeated, too, in the centerpiece, a heaping of lemons, olive branches, and grapes in a large flowerpot saucer. The antique Louis XIV photophores are of plated metal; the striped covers of the Regency chairs button down the back. To complete this harmony of colors, Dick Dumas serves a cold corn, yellow pepper, and chili soup with fresh cream — creating a wonderful shade of Naples yellow!

ISABELLE D'ORNANO

Lunch for friends from New York

For Isabelle d'Ornano, abundance and happiness go hand-in-hand. Her dining and family room, rich with objects and pictures, is the heart of the house. A chintz cloth with a large foliage design acts as background to a skillful arrangement of photographs; medallions; and Potocki, Radziwill, and Ornano family portraits. Across from these are paintings of houses—watercolors by Serebriakoff of the Potocki and Radziwill palaces—while the Louis XV cupboard hosts a collection of French and Russian silverware. Isabelle d'Ornano enjoys luncheons for six or eight people, at a round table, the ideal for conversation; for larger numbers, she prefers to set up a buffet. Flowers never appear on the table, which is covered with the same Persian fabric as the walls, but the room is delicately scented with Eau de Campagne, and the table displays a mise-en-scène of pieces: Odiot silverware with the Potocki arms in relief, not engraved; a collection of Meissen figurines representing Polish dignitaries from the Kendler period; and bronze objects by Barye. The glassware and porcelain bear the Potocki-Ornano monogram. All in all, a handsome welcome that is surely irresistible to New York friends whose visit to Isabelle d'Ornano is the first stop on their European tour.

Lunch at the office

PRIMROSE BORDIER

A touch of Zen

For a brainstorming session with her colleagues, Primrose Bordier takes her inspiration from Japan. Precision, efficiency, and an aesthetic sense are the keywords for a working lunch at which designs for a new collection of plates will be discussed. On the marble conference table, Primrose has mixed Oriental objects and homemade creations: Philippine baskets act as place plates; smaller baskets, used in Japan for hot towels, here hold the bread; there are fish-shaped chopstick-holders and Japanese porcelain bowls, as well as plates and glasses in a brush-stroke pattern by Primrose herself. At each place setting, a small bunch of white cyclamens . . . because Primrose believes in happiness at the office. And this is no doubt why she has organized this working lunch along the pleasing, somewhat ritual lines of the traditional Japanese tea ceremony.

ALAIN-DOMINIQUE PERRIN

A *must!*

Alain-Dominique Perrin has lunch in his office every day—and it is easy to see why. Why waste precious time outside when you can receive guests and colleagues in the calm of a 1930s-style Cartier maple dining room? It is an excellent opportunity to display (and also, perhaps, to test?) the latest company products. On the claret—the Cartier color—lacquered table, the president's favorite plate is laid on a linen mat that repeats the panther theme of the dinner service. Cutlery, glasses, and metal cups have all been conceived as designer labels that now adorn many households: a good idea that must have come to Alain-Dominique Perrin as he was having lunch in his office. . . .

ANDRÉE PUTMAN

Black on white

Efficient and very much in demand, Andrée Putman hates to waste a lunch hour. So, albeit with her characteristic professional discipline, she readily improvises a lunch in the showroom, using, of course, furniture and articles she has created or overseen for Écart International. On the table designed by Jacques-Henri Lartigue for his own bedroom when he was eighteen years old are mosaic-patterned plates, checkered coffee cups and saucers, and silver-and-crystal cutlery. The severe black and white is accented with childlike flights of fantasy: butterflies light on white roses from the rue Saint-Antoine market, and *loukhoum* is served in a Jean Puiforcat silver bowl. These unexpected touches are to the setting . . . what perfume is on a mysterious lady.

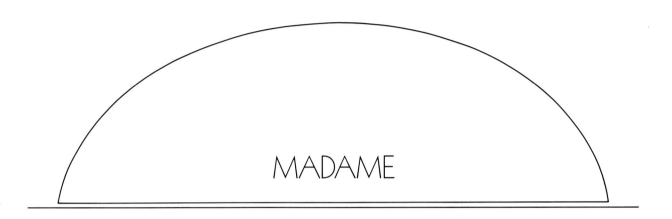

MADAME

Family mementos

When one takes tea with the Comtesse de Paris, beneath portraits of Louis-Philippe and Henri IV, with every object, piece of furniture, and painting eloquent with the history of France and the Royal Family, can one really tell whether the tea is from China or Ceylon? Whatever the case may be, it is served in white and gold porcelain cups, bearing the Orléans arms, from a design by Princesse Chantal of France for Tiffany. The silver tray with its teapot, sugar bowl, cream jug, and simple bouquet of roses, rests on Marie-Antoinette's watercolor table, made by Riesener. Can one really tell whether the tea is from China or Ceylon? . . .

DIANE
AND
ALEXANDRA DE CADAVAL

A children's party

Diane and Alexandra would be sorry to come back to Paris after their wonderful long holiday in Portugal if they weren't so happy to see all their little friends again: Tiphaine and Raphaëlle, Julie and Cornelia, Guillaume and Alexis, Luisa and Laura. One of the highlights of the end of the holidays is having them over for a children's party. This has become such a ritual that the Duchesse de Cadaval brought back from New York everything necessary for a table setting to suit the festive occasion: the paper tablecloth and napkins, the cardboard plates and cups are all strewn with colorful cats and balloons. It's a real party, with ribbons, festoons, pointed hats, surprises, and—the finishing touch—an enormous cake with cats and balloons like the tablecloth! Mint syrup and orange juice add acid shades to a table whose meticulous preparation is concealed by its deft humor—a magical memory that Diane and Alexandra will keep for a long, long time.

FRANÇOIS DURET-ROBERT

Tea at my grandmother's

When a great connoisseur like the critic and journalist François Duret-Robert decides to re-create a tea table at his grandmother's, the result might be mere art history. But it is far more, for his learning is transcended only by his passion for the turn of the century, and by the play of memories and reminiscences that are the impetus for this poetic evocation: a damask tablecloth, Majorelle plates, an Austrian silver-plated coffee set, Gallé glasses and pitcher, silver cutlery from 1900, English cups, linen napkins, and an umbellifer-shaped lamp by Maurice Bouval. François Duret-Robert seems to have achieved the "time regained" and the "contemplation of the essence of things" to which Proust referred when he related how the sound of a knife or the taste of hot herbal tea had the power to bring his Aunt Léonie's bedroom into his own.

THE DUCHESSE DE SABRAN-PONTEVÈS

In the kitchen at Ansouis

The château of Ansouis, in the department of the Vaucluse, is an ancient, tenth-century fortress whose five terraces of topiary yews overlook the Aygues valley. Largely rebuilt in the sixteenth and seventeenth centuries, the former stronghold of the sovereign comtes de Forcalquier boasts a superb blending of medieval, Renaissance, and classical—the château has been the Sabran family seat for eight centuries. The Duchesse de Sabran intends to bring the rich history of this splendid estate back to life in a book on Ansouis and the family, but she occasionally leaves her writing desk for one of her favorite pleasures: tea with her grandchildren in the castle kitchen. The kitchen was installed in vaulted medieval rooms; with its copper utensils, vast oak table, old-

fashioned stoves, and eighteenth-century Provençal furniture, it has retained its authenticity. Tea is served on an Indian-print tablecloth, with blue faience plates from Apt and an English tea set, and the children enjoy Lubéron tarts, a Cucuron specialty. Such a delightful tea enhances Ansouis's reputation for banishing sorrow — a reputation that may have its roots in the famous story of Monseigneur de Sabran, Bishop of Laon and Marie-Antoinette's confessor. Like the picture of Dorian Gray, a portrait of the bishop showed traces of the tears the bishop shed upon the death of the Queen. The right eye remained persistently red until the priest of Ansouis "exorcised" the painting, restoring to the eye its natural color.

BRUNO ROY

Masks and bergamasks

Flowers and costumes, masks and mysteries, dances and Carnival, all fascinate Bruno Roy, who loves to play in the realm of the ephemeral, the improvised, and, perhaps above all, the seductive. Here, he has used his mastery of composition to stage a brunch following the lines of a perfect pyramid. The nineteenth-century portrait is accentuated by the folds of the draped taffeta curtains and the bouquet of tulips, narcissi, broom, amaryllis, stock, and ferns, which incorporates a red and white marbled-paper Carnival mask. Organdy over striped silk covers the table, wreathed by a garland of eucalyptus caught up with large arrangements of broom, eucalyptus seeds, narcissi, and orange tulips. The plates are blue and gold porcelain, and the early-twentieth-century silverware is from Nantes—as is the Muscadet, which comes from Bruno Roy's property. As for the antique damask napkins, they bear the monogram of Roland Bonaparte and are embroidered with the Imperial crown. If chamber music were called for, it would certainly be Vinteuil's sonata. . . .

KARL LAGERFELD

White and gold suite

The fashion designer Karl Lagerfeld has employed all his artistry to produce this afternoon tea at *l'hôtel* de Maisons. His inspiration derived from the superb residence itself, which was built in the early eighteenth century and bears the name of one of its first owners, Claude de Longueil, Marquis de Maisons and President of the Parliament. The whole room, from paneling to table, is dominated by a harmony of white and gold in the soft and subtle light that filters through white taffeta curtains. The table, placed by the window and covered in damask and lace, stands on a fine Savonnerie carpet. Around an eighteenth-century gilded bronze centerpiece filled with red roses are arranged the Meissen tea set and cake dishes with gold rims and floral design; Louis XV vermeil cutlery from Puiforcat; and etched crystal glasses. Though Karl Lagerfeld takes pleasure in receiving for a high tea in this manner, though tea and chocolate, kugelhof and cake reflect his German origins, nevertheless, the way he presents them — in the unique surroundings in which Beaumarchais was entertained in times past — reveals above all the passion that has always bound him to eighteenth-century France — its grace, spirit, and achievements.

MADEMOISELLE DE . . .

Breton interlude

The terrace of this little 1880s wooden house on the Île-aux-Moines looks out on the Gulf of Morbihan. Here, they say, Mademoiselle de . . . once took refuge after a love affair with a high-ranking personage by whom she bore a son. . . . Such is the legend. But, legendary or not, those who partake of this Breton interlude will admire the late afternoon light on Dronec, Holavre, Logoden, and Hoedic islands and treat themselves to clams and oysters served with bread, salted butter, and Muscadet. The faience plates and Muscadet pitcher are by Henriot of Quimper, the fish cutlery has shell handles, and the tablecloth is batik. Some refuges are much better than others.

THE MARQUISE DE BRISSAC

After the shoot in Anjou

In Brissac, after the shoot, dinner is traditionally served early, in the vast dining room overlooked by the musicians' gallery and adorned with numerous portraits of the Nicolays, the Marquise de Brissac's ancestors. Lit by silver candelabra and surrounded by Regency chairs, the table portrays the theme of the shoot. Pheasant feathers mixed with oak leaves and cartridges are scattered on the white damask tablecloth, among the turn-of-the-century Limoges plates, the bouillon cups, and the glasses, some antique and bearing the Cossé arms, others Waterford. The white damask napkins are embroidered with the Nicolay monogram, and the wine is from the estate. The estate is fortunate: its vineyards, château, hunting, and very setting are brought alive under Jacqueline de Brissac's wise sovereignty.

Soliloquies and tête-à-têtes

GUY DE ROUGEMONT

A break at the studio

"In the beginning was color" is Guy de Rougemont's premise. But, though the color spectrum is his source of everything, it is Guy's aim to promulgate its vibrations. Color explodes on his canvases and on his urban environments, transforming a humble plate, or streaking across the most ambitious painting. And, just as naturally, color makes an appearance during the artist's break in his studio. With a single exception: the achromatic black and white tablecloth, which echoes perhaps the large stretches of bare canvas left on some of his paintings. Everything else is governed by a multicolored geometry: the chair and armchairs, inlaid with stained wood; the geometric-patterned plates; the Carrara marble candlesticks; and the bottle label designed for a Swiss vintner. Guy de Rougemont has modified even the Jean Puiforcat cutlery. Like an emblem, the three primary colors stand in three jars on a stool.

CHRISTIAN LACROIX

The first day

The first step — the first collection under his name: for Christian Lacroix, this is only the beginning. Having found for his fashion house surroundings potentially rich in symbols, his celebration here, set on a pedestal table, is almost ritualistic, its sophistication emphasized by the rubble around it. The work of Mattia Bonetti and part of a collection of furniture signed by Garouste and Bonetti, the table is of lacquered wood and is girdled by small, mercury-gilded bronze elephant heads. On the menu of this picnic launching are caviar, strawberries, and pepper vodka. Perhaps on this first day, Christian Lacroix was tempted to read his fortune in the black eggs of the sturgeon, as others do in coffee grounds or a crystal ball. Had he done so, he might have seen this miniature gala become an event in the annals of high fashion — an accession, and the first of many.

CATHERINE OF RUSSIA

An evocation by Christian Badin

As a tribute to the woman who, according to Voltaire, "placed the fine arts on her august throne," Christian Badin re-created a trompe l'oeil malachite and pink taffeta décor for one of the Pénélope shows. Standing on a hexagonal marble dais, the supper table is also draped with taffeta; the eighteenth-century bergère is of gilded wood. It is all worthy of the Empress who so appreciated the French decorative arts—suffice it to mention the "Cameos" service, Roentgen's seven trips to St. Petersburg, or the eight hundred pieces of the Orlov silver service. This table is set on a linen tablecloth with a wide hemstitched border; the cloth is embroidered with the ribbon of the Order of St. George. The same ribbon decorates the rim of the plate and the leaf-shaped dish, copies of the famous service of the Order of St. George—one of four "Order" services made by Gardner of St. Petersburg. The star of the Order of St. George shines at the centers of plate and dish, just as it shone on the chest of a Sovereign to whom Diderot attributed the "soul of Caesar" and "all the allures of Cleopatra."

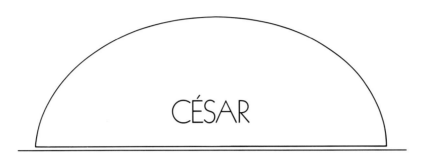

CÉSAR

Collation or collage?

Render unto Caesar what is Caesar's! Never has this saying been more apt, for when the artist César has lunch in his studio he can't but do it in the style of . . . Caesar. Thus, the following have been arranged on a soldering stone supported by a sculptor's turntable: a Provençal plate, an antique glass, an ivory-handled Hermès jackknife, an old hunting knife highly valued by the artist for cutting both his baguette and his clay, a Christofle serving fork, and a can of sardines. This is not one of the many reductions César is working on at the moment, but rather a collage. The witty composition reveals the artist's twofold nature, described by Michel Ragon as both *homo faber*, the artisan and "worker of shapes," and *homo ludens*, the playful one.

COCO CHANEL

Supper at the Ritz

This supper offers a glimpse of an era rather than a faithful reconstruction, for everyone knows that Mademoiselle Chanel always dined in rue Cambon before returning to the Ritz to sleep. All this only adds to the legend, and Marie-Caroline Bourrellis and Blandine Leroy will surely be forgiven this minor distortion of historical fact. Along with Claude de Lupia, Marie-Caroline and Blandine were able to assemble several of Mademoiselle Chanel's belongings, among them, some of the signature pieces of her fashion house: the famous quilted shoulder bag, the bottle of No. 5, the personal plates decorated with Coco Chanel's monogram—beautifully set off on the linen tablecloth embroidered by Pénélope—a large white bouquet like the ones she loved, her sable wrap, and her pearls. "Ambience is everything."

ATALANTA DE CASTELLANE

A jewel-case for a supper

Using thick carpets, hangings, padding and trimmings, gilded bronze and crystal, interior designer Atalanta de Castellane recently re-created, for Puiforcat, the atmosphere of a nine-teenth-century supper—a décor as sumptuous as a jewel-case. A worthy setting, indeed, for two rarities: the nine-teenth-century Baccarat crystal chairs, exquisitely fashioned and covered with a padded velvet in the same red as the wall hangings and the velvet curtains. On the Russian table of cut glass and bronze are laid blue and gold porcelain plates, vermeil place plates and cutlery by Puiforcat, and Baccarat glasses. This astonishing and brilliant décor, all mixture and extravagance, inspires one to modify Jules Renard's aphorism: "Style is the rejection of all styles."

MADAMA BUTTERFLY

An evocation by Chiyoko Motono

The *Abraham Lincoln,* the ship that is bringing Pinkerton back, has just arrived in Nagasaki harbor. Cio-Cio-San, who never doubted his fidelity, awaits him, and this is the supper she has prepared for his return. Such is the scene by Chiyoko Motono, the interior designer and daughter of the Japanese ambassador to Paris, for one of the Pénélope shows. As in Puccini's music, Japanese themes and Western art combine—around a lavish tablecloth dotted with butterflies—a large Japanese screen, place plates, vegetable dish, candelabrum, Puiforcat vermeil cutlery, plates with golden butterflies on the rims, crystal pitcher and glasses. The bouquet here is not of the cherry-tree branches that inspired the famous "Flower Duet" of the second act, but of chrysanthemums and gypsophilas, as if the designer, foreshadowing *Madama Butterfly*'s final tragedy, preferred to evoke the decline of autumn rather than the joy of spring.

EUGÈNE DE BEAUHARNAIS

An evocation by Pierre-Hervé Walbaum

Eugène de Beauharnais was a son worthy of his mother, the Empress Josephine. From her, he inherited a taste for splendor and sophistication, favoring severe yet sumptuous décors, like the one for this supper in *l'hôtel* Beauharnais, re-created by Pierre-Hervé Walbaum for one of the Pénélope shows. All the furniture and other pieces are by great manufacturers: the bed is by Molitor, the fruit bowl by Odiot, the cheval glass by Jacob; the torchères, by Percier and Fontaine, were made for Madame Récamier. The bouillotte lamp is a model made by Biennais for the Emperor Napoleon I, although its Imperial emblems were subsequently replaced with those of King Louis-Philippe. The table is draped with an embroidered lawn tablecloth by Pénélope and laid with vermeil and delightful hand-painted plates by Edward Memory. A charming detail: on this particular evening, a sauce for the asparagus was served in vermeil and silver oysters.

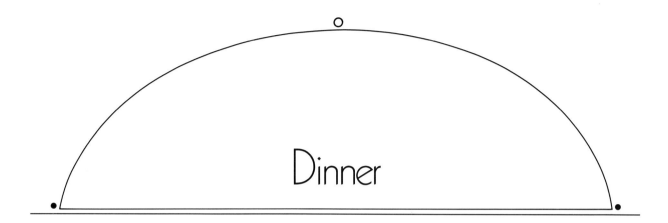

JEAN PUIFORCAT

An evocation by Éliane Scali

Whereas Pascal opposed the spirit of geometry to the spirit of finesse, Jean Puiforcat combined them both ably and admirably. At once gifted with a mathematician's great precision and a sculptor's tactile and sensual sensitivity, he was above all fascinated by the absolute. As for Éliane Scali, she displays the spirit of fidelity in this dining room re-created for Pénélope, in which, in the words of the great goldsmith himself, "the proportions are determined by the heart." The works of art, furniture, and other pieces form a whole that banishes the superfluous and the gratuitous. On the rosewood Dominique table, around a stunning luminous frosted-glass centerpiece, the silver- and gold-rimmed porcelain and the solid-silver cutlery are the ones used by Jean Puiforcat himself. A canvas by Gromaire, sconces by Gaëtan Lanzini, a carpet by Paule Leleu, a bust by Jean Puiforcat, glasses by Lalique . . . The fusion is so complete that the boundaries between functional objects and artistic creations blur. As Jean Puiforcat said so well: "A teapot is a work of art that must, in its modest sphere, elevate the soul with its beauty."

THE BARON
ÉRIC DE ROTHSCHILD

The treasures of Château-Lafite

Emblazoned with a double seal—for Château-Lafite, one of the world's finest vineyards, and for the Rothschild family—the dining room at Lafite, pale green with white paneling, seems conceived to celebrate a unique and marvelous experience. The "Vieux Bordeaux" porcelain service, pink, turquoise, and green, and bearing the double R of the Rothschilds, was custom-made for Baronne James in 1868. The delicacy of its paste and colors, and the extraordinary variety of its pieces are echoed in the Beauvais-stitch embroidered tablecloth, designed twenty years ago by Madame Porthault. Éric de Rothschild, who now rules Château-Lafite, gathers his guests around the vast table, overlooked by a bust of Baron James. Though the setting in every way follows the great traditions of entertaining in France and the Médoc, the silverware, nineteenth-century Baccarat etched glasses, Biedermeier chairs, the simple bouquets of roses from the garden, and the fruit bowls full of grapes are all subtle personal touches that, with the discretion proper to objects of quality, leave the starring role to the porcelain. At the dessert course, the famous "Châteaux" service will display all the great estates of the region.

NICOLE TOUSSAINT DU WAST

An air of opera

Nicole Toussaint du Wast's house is truly astonishing. Quintessentially nineteenth century, it is a spectacular place that allows one's spirit to breathe. Its theatricality ceases to surprise when one learns that it was entirely designed by Charles Garnier, the architect of the Paris Opéra. Built for the Luzarches d'Azay, it was resold, still unfinished, to Léopold Bourlon de Rouvres, prefect to Napoleon III, who asked Garnier to undertake the interior decoration as well. The architect threw himself enthusiastically into the task, as evidenced by the Córdoba imitation leather on the walls, the monumental—and purely decorative—fireplace of imitation stone and gold stucco, and the green velvet brocade curtains and upholstery of the chairs, which date from 1870. The whole is a masterpiece of the Napoleon III style and the ideal setting for a literary and artistic *salon*. Indeed, Nicole Toussaint du Wast often entertains famous writers (many of them members of the Académie Française), great musicians, and renowned historians. Michel Mohrt, André Castelot, Ghislain de Diesbach, Jean Dutourd, Marcel Schneider, Raymond Gallois-Montbrun, Henri Sauguet will dine at a macramé tablecloth, using Paris porcelain plates decorated with scenes of Napoleon I's battles. The very fine eighteenth-century tumbler-shaped etched glasses and the English silverware with historiated handles depicting hunting scenes are reminders that the mistress of the house is a passionate collector of anything that suits her . . . opera house! As she once said at a ball she hosted there, "The décor of the house even disguised those who weren't in costume!"

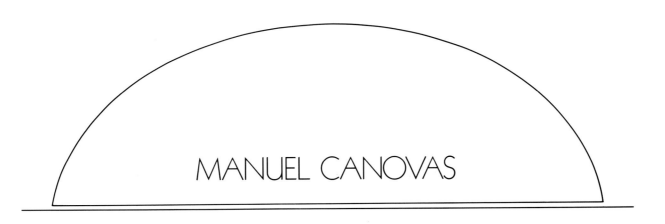

MANUEL CANOVAS

A sunlight dinner

Museums are already recognizing Manuel Canovas's mastery of color. From his earliest fabric designs, he has consistently devised new harmonies and produced daring new patterns. According to him, there are no ugly colors, only displeasing combinations. Thus, when he composes a dinner table, he does so somewhat as a great "nose" develops a new perfume: he brings out one color with the help of another, tempers this one with that, and adds a resonance of color to his finest objects that makes them stand out even more. This table is laid in the living room, which is reserved for special occasions such as a birthday dinner. The sunny feeling derives from the yellow moiré walls, the mauve tablecloth, and the pink accents provided by the scenes decorating the superb Niderwiller ice buckets and the phalaenopsis branches placed in antique Lalique bottles. The plates are by Manuel with his family's arms, and the cutlery has lapis lazuli handles. Because of its luminous colors, we shall call the setting a "sunlight dinner."

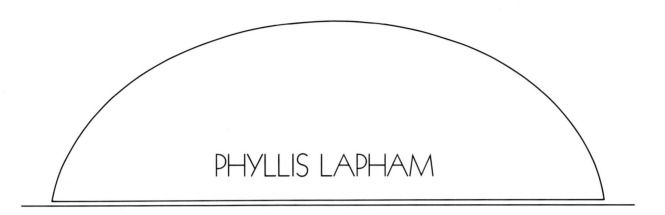

PHYLLIS LAPHAM

An American in Paris

Both passion and necessity motivate Phyllis Lapham's trips from East to West and West to East. The California-based interior designer and antiques dealer cannot do without Paris and spends six weeks there three times a year looking for bargains and entertaining friends. But, though she shuttles between Carmel, Pebble Beach, and the eighth *arrondissement,* she knows no frontiers and is as drawn to the decorative arts of the Far East as she is to those of Europe. The dining room, hung with a blue-on-blue Chinese-motif cotton, accommodates both a large eighteenth-century Japanese screen and an early-nineteenth-century Austrian chandelier. On the table, encircled by eighteenth-century Dutch lacquered chairs, are nineteenth-century Japanese Imari plates on silver place plates, English silverware, Baccarat and blue Bristol glasses, silver candelabra by Edward Wakelin, and a silver tureen from Augsburg. The sophisticated nocturnal ambience unifies this combination, artfully arranged by a true citizen of the world.

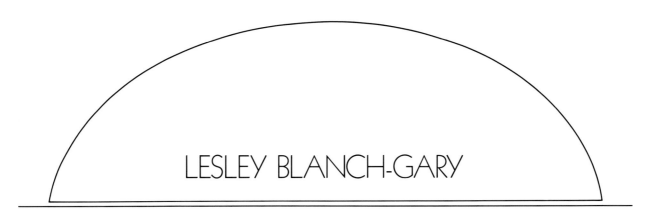

LESLEY BLANCH-GARY

The romantic study

Loaded with treasures and humming with stories, the caravan has just arrived: this is the impression one comes away with, after a visit to Lesley Blanch's home in the south of France. The English author's many books include her most famous, *The Wilder Shores of Love,* and a recent biography of Pierre Loti. The former wife of Romain Gary, and a friend of Nancy Mitford and Peter Ustinov, she is fascinated by Russia, the East, and Islam. In her home, books, cats, incense, and souvenirs from Turkey, the Balkans, Afghanistan, the Persian Gulf, and the desert all create a bohemian and cosmopolitan atmosphere. There is no dining room as such, but in the library, up against the books, a table is laid with pieces from all over the world. The plates are from upper Provence, the tablecloth is of Genoa voile, the straw mats are Chinese, and the silver tumblers and jug and wooden lacquered spoons are from Russia. The napkins are handkerchiefs bought in the marketplace at Aleppo, and the Arcopal borscht bowls are from the local five-and-ten. In the middle of the table is a head of broccoli in a straw basket. There are two carafes, one always topped with a lemon, the other with an orange—a custom as personal as the way Lesley Blanch uses the Chinese bell: she rings it loudly, not to call the servants, but to change a conversation that does not interest her.

MR. AND MRS. DAVID OGILVY

The colors of Touffou

The relationship between David Ogilvy, the "pope of advertising," and Touffou, the "château the color of the setting sun," is a love affair more than twenty years old. Celebrated by Ronsard and honored by a visit from François I in February 1541, Touffou is reflected in the waters of the Vienne. The steep roofs on the eleventh- , fourteenth- , and sixteenth-century sections of the castle have been completely rebuilt, one by one, by David Ogilvy. Whether she is receiving the roofers who have just—after seven years of work—dismantled the last piece of scaffolding, or hosting a meeting of the heads of the many subsidiaries of the Ogilvy & Mather agency, Herta Ogilvy prepares an equally magnificent setting. On a large mahogany table, surrounded by medallion chairs, the tone is set by the "Fitzhugh Pattern" Chinese Export dinner service. Everything is determinedly, perfectly, strictly blue and white, a one-color show typical of David Ogilvy's style. After all, he is well acquainted with the virtues of originality, having tirelessly challenged the commonplaces of advertising with an independent mind and an infallible sense of paradox. A Madison Avenue star and the author of remarkable *Confessions,* at Touffou he is also a gardener when the fancy takes him, raising antique varieties of roses in a series of secret gardens.

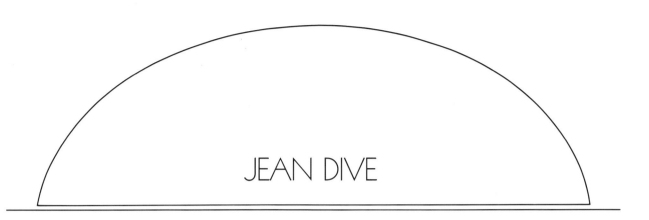

JEAN DIVE

A private dining room

The atmosphere of Jean Dive's apartment is deeply colored and intimate. It is an apartment for evenings, when the interior designer likes to entertain a few close friends in this tiny alcove, as comfortable and warm as it is well conceived. The padded banquette conveys the feeling of a private dining room, its quiet atmosphere conducive to conversation. The red carpet and the blue and red chintz on the walls harmonize subtly with the double Souleiado tablecloth. A paler shade of blue and more red echo in the Provençal soft-paste porcelain plates, blue plastic cutlery, and Biot glasses of the table setting. The small loaves come from a nearby restaurant, Chiberta, which Jean Dive designed and still frequents. In the center of the table, depending on the number of guests or his own inspiration, Jean Dive places either a single photophore — its base wreathed with anemones, tulips, and chrysanthemum-daisies — or else two storm glasses placed over blue and white Chinese porcelain vases. Above the English mahogany console table is a small collection of nineteenth-century canvases of fruits and vegetables. In the recess, gouaches of Naples and Venice act as openings in a pleasantly enclosed world.

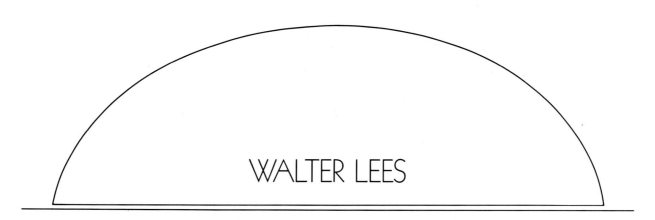

WALTER LEES

A princely kitchen

In the nineteenth century, it was the done thing to have a *salon,* whether literary or purely social. Walter Lees appears to be continuing this tradition, except that his *salon* is in fact a kitchen— and many of the world's great have dined in this blue, gold, and crystal kitchen. A masterpiece of organization, refined sophistication, and light, the kitchen is also the real heart of this gifted host's tiny apartment. The long, narrow table is covered with white damask and laid with blue and white porcelain, vermeil, and silver. There are "Blue Dragon" Worcester plates, Augsburg candlesticks, early-seventeenth-century English snuff- and candy boxes, a muffin dish, and Venetian glasses. The Venetian salad plates are based on a Louis XIV model; the carafes are Tiffany wine decanters. This kitchen is a worthy *salon* indeed!

ALAIN DEMACHY

Through the looking glass

As an experienced antiques dealer and interior designer, Alain Demachy collects ideas as well as pieces in his distant travels. But, though fascinated by the Orient and the Indies, he remains elegantly European and true to his classical taste. In the dining room, the low table, Moroccan-style poufs, and nocturnal atmosphere suggest magic and foreign parts, while the harmony of tones, and the arrangement of the table and of the numerous objects evoke a more familiar world. Around the low table, the banquette and poufs are all upholstered in Thai silk by Jim Thompson. On the predominantly deep-blue tablecloth are laid Minton plates on vermeil place plates, the family silver, and the most delicate Baccarat crystal glasses. The silk velvet on the wall sets off a handsome collection of mirrors: small triangular mirrors by Emilio Terry, sixteenth-century Venetian mirrors with *églomisé* frames, of amber and tortoiseshell. In the center is a gold and turquoise Tibetan necklace. With such a mix of dreams, reflections, and reality, it is not always easy to tell which side of the mirror we are on. . . .

ALBERTO PINTO

A fine anniversary

Three tables, thirty guests, two hundred white tulips, and dozens of camellias—Alberto Pinto seems to be drawing from a horn of plenty to celebrate thirty years of Hubert de Givenchy's fashion designs. The party is held in the dining room of Paul Morand's former apartment, a white monochrome, its mother-of-pearl and ivory echoed by Bruno Roy's floral artistry. On the Syrian pieces flanking the Louis XIV marble fireplace, two huge bouquets of one hundred white tulips bloom from Givenchy hatboxes, tissue paper, and ribbons. On the tables, moss trees sport camellias, while on white damask tablecloths are mixed silver Napoleon III place plates, small seventeenth-century candlesticks, vermeil and silver cutlery, and Venetian glasses. The setting displays Alberto Pinto's natural generosity, enhanced by his exquisite sense of harmony.

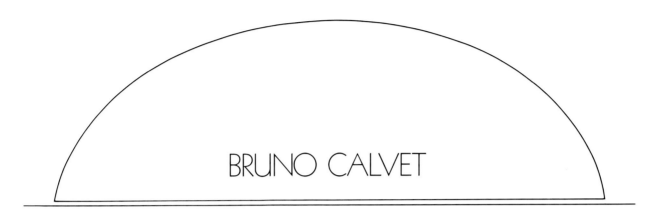

BRUNO CALVET

Surprises in a Bordeaux cupboard

Some hold the silverware and are only opened on feast days, others smell of lavender and clean linen. Bruno Calvet's Bordeaux cupboard, with its collection of eighteenth-century Bordeaux faience, is always open to our admiring eyes. The focal piece of the small dining room, it is full of endless surprises. There are tobacco jars, trivets, *tulipières,* feeding-cups, clogs, jugs, dishes, and little boxes. On the table, which is also faience, are individual *rafraîchissoirs,* for rinsing one's glass between wines; plates from the "au Dauphin" service decorated with shields bearing the French arms; and an oval tureen in the so-called Manganese Rose style, with its branch-and-insect decoration. Real roses are scattered on the table—perfect complements to such a collection.

MADAME JEAN AMIC

Fruit, flowers, leaves, branches

There are many candles in this summer dining room, because Irène Amic could not bring herself to sacrifice the beauty of her splendid Charles X décor to the comforts of electricity. The Empire chandelier and candelabra illuminate this classically proportioned room, while flowers and leaves on table and walls combine in a veritable bouquet of perfumes and colors. The roses, peaches, and apricots are framed by garlands of ivy, nineteenth-century Minton plates, and mahogany chairs, each with a different tapestry design. The cut glass is Baccarat, the large damask napkins embroidered with the monogram of the Cantacuzènes, Irène Amic's ancestors. How fortunate that the Wicked Electricity Fairy is powerless against the subtle charm of this setting!

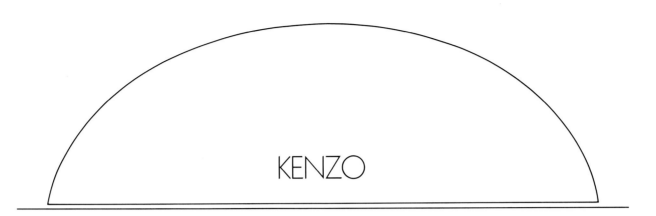

KENZO

In *haiku* form

The carp gave a leap
and the water still once more—
the cuckoo sings

Everything here recalls the *haiku*, that short, strictly ruled Japanese poem that can wondrously evoke an instant and an eternity. Here, there is perfection of detail, simplicity of construction, poetic expression, and even bareness, as if Kenzo Takada wanted a respite from the colors he uses so generously in his creations. In front of carp leaping on a nineteenth-century silk Kno screen, the table has been laid on a Venetian white damask cloth, itself draped over a Japanese undercloth. The antique Japanese plates are blue and white, as are the bowls and the *sake* goblets, the latter decorated with the "tako" octopuses that Kenzo collects. The only verticals are the two Japanese bronze candlesticks with bases in the form of monkeys, and the Venetian glasses from Murano, made especially for Kenzo by Gino Senedese. In the center of the table, in a leaf-shaped jardinière, are a water-lily leaf and a white amaryllis. With white, blues, and natural tints, the great Japanese fashion designer—so Parisian in his lively and colorful style—seems to have found once more the spiritual inwardness of Japanese homes. In the words of Okakura Kakuzo's little *Book of Tea:* "True beauty can only be discovered by one who has mentally completed the incomplete."

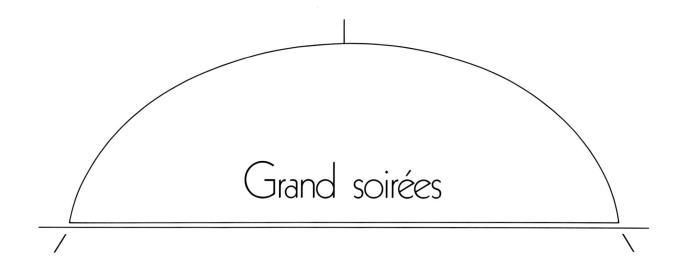

Grand soirées

LAURA
AND
CORINNE MENTZELOPOULOS

The roses of Margaux

Honor to whom honor is due! Château-Margaux is, first and foremost, the greatest vineyard of the illustrious Margaux family of wines, but it is, as well, a very handsome home that seems to work a kind of spell on all who behold it. Built in 1810 by Louis Combes for the passionate Marquis de Colonilla, it has sheltered important personalities ever since — both Aguado, Rossini's patron, and the great Fernand Ginestet, an outstanding Bordeaux figure, lived here. Today, the Mentzelopouloses have given a new impetus to the estate with the recently completed and delightful restoration of the park and château. In the dining room, with its trompe l'oeil marble walls and Egyptian-style stove, the table resembles a garden, strewn as it is with fifty white roses in fifty bud vases, gracefully mingling with Meissen figurines. In front of each guest are five glasses: for water, white wine, two red Bordeaux wines, and a Sauterne. Among the three different porcelain services, the cheese plates, copies of the "Châteaux" service, portray Château-Margaux. The Odiot silverware and vermeil are in the style of the Margaux period. Upon Empire console tables, the superb gilded bronze epergnes filled with the first fruits of the grape harvest could almost be symbols of the château considered by many the Versailles of the Médoc.

MONSIEUR
AND
MADAME CHARLES DE YTURBE

At the table of Diane of Poitiers

Diane, dressed in her customary black and white, might have just left this table, re-created every year in her honor by Charles de Yturbe in the castle of Anet. Everything here evinces the "Grande Sénéschale"; every object once belonged to her and has a history—or a tale—attached to it. The sumptuous silver nefs were once filled with wine and rolled from guest to guest; silver German wedding cups portray a married couple; the Venetian glasses, they say, were molded on her breast. The carafes were presented to her upon her arrival in Lyons in 1550, and are etched with the famous monogram that caused Catherine de' Medici so much anguish, for she never knew if Henri II's initial was entwined with the crescent of his device—or with the D of Diane. After the King's death, the "Lady of the Harts" retired to Anet, where she had so well employed the services of Jean Goujon, Philibert Delorme, Benvenuto Cellini, and others. One day she entertained, likely at this table, a certain nobleman by the name of Brantôme who was to add the finishing touch to her legend. Bewitched by her beauty, he was to write that "every morning, she drank infusions of liquid gold."

HÉLÈNE ROCHAS

Elective affinities

It is as if La Bruyère whispered to Hélène Rochas that "the most refined pleasure is to give pleasure to others." But Mme Rochas, for whom the heart is the surest guide, has no need to be reminded. Indeed, she follows her heart in composing magnificent tables, delightful soirées, and intimate parties for intimate friends. For them alone she assembles her most prized possessions in her white-paneled dining room, and for these occasions excels in creating exclusive environments based on almost coded exchanges between initiates. This impression is reinforced by the décor, which partakes of both an art-lover's collection and a conclave of grand electors. There are stunning Gérard Mille chairs (with white lacquer, green leather, and high backs), overdoors and overmantel by Serebriakoff (a trompe l'oeil of Chinese porcelain and Iznik, Mishapor, and Samarkand faience), and Thomire candelabra. And, because she knows that affinities between objects, as between people, arise from a mysterious attraction rather than from superficial similarity, Hélène Rochas readily juxtaposes French and English silverware, Venetian tumblers, eighteenth-century Delft vases, a mounted seventeenth-century Japanese porcelain, and an embroidered Italian tablecloth. How can one say whether she chooses her favorite objects for her most precious friends—or her most precious objects for her favorite friends?

MADAME MICHEL DAVID-WEILL

Sceaux quartet

Four tables and four colors grace this dinner given by Hélène David-Weill at her rue Saint-Guillaume mansion. Built in the late seventeenth century for the Marquis de Laigue, it received Lamartine on his return from the East and today is one of the last Parisian *hôtels* to be occupied by a single family. The seating plans are displayed around the equestrian bronze of Louis XIV, on a pedestal table with porphyry top in the large entrance hall. In the dining room, the four tables are framed by the room's wood paneling and pale green stucco. Each has a different bouquet, arranged by the majordomo to further emphasize the beauty and rarity of the faience plates from Sceaux, with their serrate edges and variety of flowers painted in the centers. The lawn tablecloths, the doilies for the bread plates, and the napkins are all embroidered with flowers. The silverware is Puiforcat, the glasses Lalique. If Renan, who once lived here, had seen this décor, he would have been bolstered in his credo that "France has exquisite taste!"

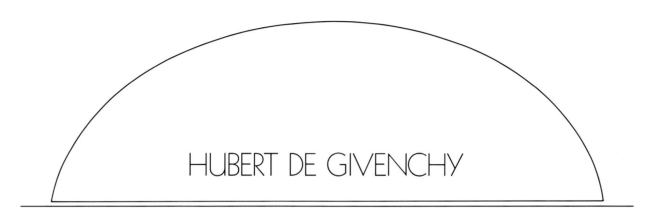

HUBERT DE GIVENCHY

Golden number

For the fashion designer as for the architect, a sense of proportion is the principal goal. Hubert de Givenchy achieves this balance, this elegance of proportion, in all things, whether he is furnishing a room, combining colors, or blending subtlety and simplicity. He acknowledges no boundaries: the creator's art is also the art of living. Here, his sense of harmony is revealed by the soft, almost beige, off-white of the linen tablecloth, which complements the paneling perfectly. Here are both grandeur and simplicity—the apposition of a Regency tureen and pots of helxine and orchids. The tones are balanced—the green of the taffeta curtains, the gold of the Gouthière candlesticks, the mahogany of the Roentgen rolltop desk, and the muted leather of the Louis XVI chairs, all enhanced by the Hubert Robert painting. Finally, there is the choice of materials—the silver of the English plates and the eighteenth-century cutlery, the crystal of the Marquise Nagliati glasses, the mahogany, the bronze, the marble. . . . All this is achieved by Hubert de Givenchy's rare gift of knowing how to make the simple sublime and the sublime simple.

THE BARONNE GUY DE ROTHSCHILD

A lordly dinner at *l'hôtel* Lambert

At the magical moment when the prow-shaped bow window above the Quai d'Anjou merges with the night, a thousand candles light up the Hercules Gallery of *l'hôtel* Lambert. This evening, Marie-Hélène de Rothschild is giving a dinner for forty-six. Under the wonderful Le Brun ceiling, she has arranged everything with infinite care, raising the tiniest detail to the level of a small masterpiece. Perfect bows fasten white linen tablecloths over the sideboards; there are yellow and white bouquets; the folding chairs are padded with red damask. Were Bacchus and Pan to prepare a banquet in the heavens, the opulence of this earthly table would surely rival it! The three Sèvres dinner services, Louis XIV glasses, eighteenth-century silverware, and vermeil dessert cutlery are in perfect harmony with the gilded paneling, the Italian ebony cabinets, and the fine damask stools. It is as if the Baronne de Rothschild allowed herself to be secretly guided by the heroes of Van Obstal and Le Brun. France is fortunate that heads of households such as the Baronne perpetuate so brilliantly the art of entertaining. . . .

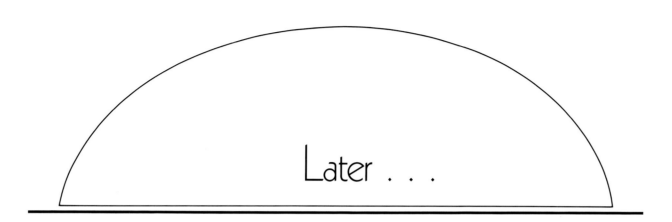

Later . . .

CHARLOTTE AILLAUD

Pre-concert drinks

What better prelude to music—at the Opéra or a *lundi de l'Athénée*—than to gather around a glass served by François-Xavier Lalanne's dramatic cat? A strange animal of repoussé brass, this bar was ordered by Émile Aillaud in 1968, and combines a fish's tail, a bird's wings, and a cat's head. It is very large, almost preposterously so, a surrealistic note in an otherwise strictly classical décor. Behind the wings are hidden a few of the hostess' collections, in particular, eighteenth-century Portuguese glasses, Dominici carafes with silver-plated necks, and Venetian glassware. After such a spectacular introduction, the transition to the opera and its strange creatures will be a natural one.

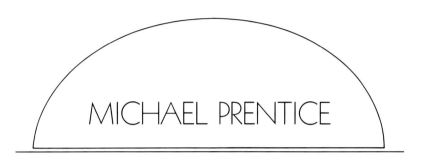

MICHAEL PRENTICE

The *Commendatore's* feast

"Don Giovanni, a cenar teco m'invitasti . . ."—"Don Giovanni, you invited me to dinner." One almost expects to hear the *Commendatore* knocking, so imposing is the granite block that the sculptor Michael Prentice has made into a table. The similarities are not merely formal, for here, as in Mozart's opera, spiritual and physical realities echo one another. Impressive as it is, the mass of South African black granite incorporates everything necessary for a feast: a sink, a lemon squeezer, three gas rings, a grater, a tap, saltcellars, and a grinder. Leporello would be delighted! The nineteenth-century Italian silver candlesticks illuminate the banquet, which tonight consists of oysters, to be eaten with striking eighteenth-century shellfish-forks with ivory handles. *"A cenar teco m'invitasti, e son venuto"*—"Here I am, I have come," announces the *Commendatore.* Pierre Jean Jouve's insightful comment comes to mind: "The weight and coldness of stone, together with the proud rigidity of bronze and, too, the inexplicable majesty of the soul, have changed the proportion of all things."

LA TRAVIATA

An evening at Violetta's

That evening, on the stage of the Paris Opéra, Violetta was Cecilia Gasdia, under the direction of Zubin Mehta in a production by Zeffirelli. But this gala dinner—with setting by François Catroux and flowers by Bruno Roy—so approached the magnificence of the great first-act feast of *La Traviata* that the guests could well have burst into "Libiamo ne' lieti calici"! It was all pelmets on the balconies, shades on the candelabra, and an immense train of flowers up the main staircase, a profusion of amaryllis, plum-tree branches, euphorbias, hyacinths, Guernsey lilies, and gypsophilas. The tables were covered with orange-red cloths, the candelabra decorated with camellias tied with satin bows. In a moment, Gastone will introduce Alfredo to Violetta. . . .

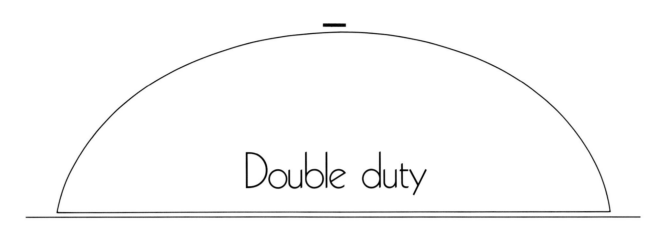

THE COMTESSE
JEAN DE ROHAN-CHABOT

Chromatic fancies

Joy de Rohan-Chabot is such an enthusiastic painter that she decorates everything she touches. The screen, table, and walls of her charming little Parisian home all belong to the domain of pure fancy, and are a triumph of color. Joy entertains guests for lunch in her winter garden, luxuriant with floral themes. On the table, painted in a fern-and-primrose design, is a whimsically heterogeneous collection: 1940s Vallauris plates, slipware, Biot glasses, "mismatched" cutlery — ivory-handled knives, bamboo-pattern spoons, and silver forks — even the centerpiece mixes primroses and anemones. Evenings, the table, with its cashmere and Indian coverings, is laid in the entrance. The Chinese Export plates find a remarkable echo in the two screens that Joy painted with trompe l'oeil dishes and plates, after going to China to learn the technique of lacquering. The glasses and carafes are etched with the family arms. There are eighteenth-century forks, a branch of cymbidium in a Japanese porcelain vase, and antique saltcellars. Joy creates a slightly crazy but supremely stylish atmosphere; she invents, paints, and enjoys herself. . . .

THE PRIME MINISTER
AND
MADAME JACQUES CHIRAC

At *l'hôtel* Matignon

L'hôtel Matignon, the residence of prime ministers since 1935, has managed to be a true home for its occupants as well. Its French elegance and sophistication are ideally suited to both large, official dinners and informal luncheons. At this lunch, Jacques and Bernadette Chirac are entertaining eight guests in the first-floor dining room. The oval table is covered with a Pénélope tablecloth embroidered with phalaenopsis, while a springtime centerpiece accords perfectly with a porcelain service decorated with a delicate leaf design and custom-made for Matignon. In the evening, forty-five guests attend an official dinner in the splendid, gold and white paneled Salle du Conseil on the ground floor. The immense table is covered with white damask, and adorned with a multitude of round bouquets of freesias, tulips, buttercups, cornflowers, viburnums, and hyacinths. The Sèvres "Matignon" porcelain plates, with their gray and gold Empire pattern, and the Christofle silverware, engraved with the R. F. monogram of the French Republic, were created especially for the rue de Varenne. But whatever the time or the season, one of the great pleasures for the Prime Minister's guests is the wonderful park, which, in the words of Jean Courtonne, the architect of Matignon, delights the spectator "with its layout and the beauty of its views of all that is most cheerful in the environs of Paris."

MADAME DIDIER WIRTH

Summertime, wintertime

Sameness breeds boredom, they say. Barbara Wirth takes this saying to heart: not content with changing her table setting, she varies her entire dining room according to the season, from green's summer freshness to red's winter warmth. In the summer version, the dining room walls are tiled in pale green, and the blinds and chairs are covered in hand-painted geraniums, clematis, camellias, and single roses. The tablecloths are batik, the napkins of green and pink linen, and the green-striped carpet of coconut matting. Everything is fresh or transparent: antique glasses, Moustiers faience with trompe l'oeil vegetables, baskets of red fruit and mixed herbs, a collection of antique carafes and Diego Giacometti storm lamps.

197

In winter, by contrast, the tone is consistently warm. The walls are covered in panels of fabric with small red and white chevrons. The blinds and chairs are red, and the tablecloths are red linen over batik. Chinese plates, antique silverware, and red carafes are arranged around large bouquets of bellflowers. On the mantel, a collection of glasses includes some rare blue fennels. Barbara Wirth, whose taste is rooted in the tradition of the decorative arts, might here be suggesting a modern version of the eighteenth-century changes in décor — "summer furniture, winter furniture."

MONSIEUR AND MADAME ÉMILE GARCIN

A scent *à la* Mistral

Imbued with the atmosphere of a turn-of-the-century Provençal family home, this house was a fine discovery for Émile Garcin, familiar as he is with the narrowest back roads and the most secluded properties of the region. And, since it is difficult to seek dream homes for others without looking out for bargains for oneself, the Garcins have gathered their numerous finds here. In the kitchen, these comprise the small pieces of Provençal furniture; the wine-vat tiles that cover the kitchen stove; the flour, salt, and olive oil pots; an antique piece of furniture once used by a grain merchant; and the flowers and herbs that Estelle Garcin hangs up to dry from the ceiling. In the dining room, the two hundred or so turn-of-the-century plates and dishes are pleasingly arranged on shelving designed by Émile Garcin. In both rooms monochrome tableware is laid on a red tablecloth. The brown Gien service matches the tones of the Provençal pottery on the checked oilcloth in the kitchen. On the printed tablecloth in the dining room, the small slipware plates, the napkins, and a large Provençal tureen are all green. The light of the surrounding countryside seems to add to all these colors what the southern accent adds to the French language—an enchanting vibration.

HÉLÈNE BOUILLOUX-LAFONT

Sunday in the country

It is a fine day, and the French windows of Hélène's bedroom are wide open onto the garden. Very early in the morning she went out to pick roses and fetch warm brioches and croissants from the village. Now, breakfast is served; the houseguests join her. The blue china, the strawberry teapot, and the leaf dishes outdo one another in charm and whimsy — a natural and spontaneous whimsy that will be the order of the day. In the late morning, when friends call up and invite themselves for lunch, Hélène improvises at a long stone table on the terrace. Suddenly, there appear pyramids of fruit, salads, chilled wine in Sarreguemines carafes, Portuguese glasses, and a blue china bowl. Tumblers are amusingly arranged on a rack for draining bottles. People help themselves and sit down where they like — on the sunny terrace, in the shade of the trees, in a deckchair, or under the umbrella. Truly, a feast for the eyes!

JACQUELINE HAGNAUER

Town and country

In her house in Provence, Jacqueline Hagnauer likes to choose between recapturing her Parisian spirit and creating an entirely bucolic atmosphere. The choice depends on her mood and on her guests. She sets both kinds of table with the same sophisticated eye and sensitivity for objects that have made her such a successful antiques dealer. In the town version, a cashmere tablecloth sets off the nineteenth-century English Derby plates and the trios of glasses at each place—a Bohemian water glass, a blue Napoleon III glass, and an etched glass. At the center of the table, a silver pumpkin holding small containers for condiments is surrounded by bunches of freesias and hydrangeas, English candlesticks, blue Bristol glass saltshakers, and individual woven-silver bread baskets. The fish knives and forks are English; the napkins are of green linen. In the country version, the table is covered with a green and pink Indian print and is cheerful with flowers and fruit, both real and artificial: bunches of roses from the garden, small slipware plates resting on "Pont-aux-Choux" place plates, and a witty basket of cherries, also of slipware. Here, the trios of glasses pick up the dominant pink, green, and white of the table. Town table or country table—how delightful to know they are both in the country, so that no noise will disturb the party. . . .

SHEILA DE ROCHAMBEAU

Pumpkin story

Since she likes both to cook and to enjoy her friends' company, Sheila de Rochambeau decided to do both at once. And so this cozy room—half kitchen, half dining room—came to be. The room, in shades of Naples yellow and *crème brûlée,* is a treat in itself, created by Sheila. Today's main theme is the pumpkin. A whole one holds pride of place, its muted, rusty hue determining the colors of the lunch table. There are trompe l'oeil marble plates, a printed patchwork tablecloth, English silverware, *faux* tortoiseshell Italian tumblers, linen napkins; the superb carafes are magnum decanters. In the evening, the hollowed-out pumpkin is filled with flowers. On the coral-colored linen tablecloth are eighteenth-century English plates, French silver candlesticks, and small individual carafes. In such a gastronomic atmosphere, the pumpkin requires that the guests conclude the evening listening to Teresa Berganza sing arias from the opera *La Cenerentola.*

THE BARON DE CONDÉ

Tables of harmony

"Objects, settings, houses, gardens—he has the gift of knowing them, appreciating them, arranging them, and loving them. Harmony is his business." This is from Maurice Druon's preface to the catalogue of an exhibition of the painter Alain de Condé's work. Whether he is entertaining friends for dinner around the fireplace during the wine harvest, or re-creating the theme of a canvas in the garden, Alain de Condé proceeds with the same innate finesse, the same sense of right relations between things. In the kitchen, a fire fueled with vine shoots blazes. On the checked mats—handkerchiefs bought at the market of Castillon-la-Bataille, near Saint-Émilion—is a Gien service from 1860 that bears the Condé arms; there are glasses for Bordeaux, eighteenth-century white-wine glasses, Portuguese molded glass tumblers, family silverware, and antique silver candlesticks. On the wall is a collection of still lifes by Bordeaux artists of the eighteenth and nineteenth centuries, and over the fireplace are some superb "Vieux Bordeaux" dishes. To the right of the fireplace is the stone stove—an early ancestor of the kitchen range. Outside, the painter has re-created the theme of one of his recent canvases. The frame is the inner courtyard of his house, full of flowers that he grows himself: asters, begonias, lavender, morning glories, blue water lilies, and oleanders, among many others. The subject is a table, covered with a blue and white cloth, with silver coffeepot and basket of fruit. How accurately Maurice Druon says of Alain de Condé that "his painting is, in a way, a thanksgiving, which is the quality of its light."

Details

COVER
Tablecloth, Pénélope* / place plates and vermeil bowl and saltshaker, Puiforcat / Victorian vermeil cutlery from Véronique Girard / eighteenth-century glasses from Philippe Leroux.

14 THE BARONNE GÉRARD DE WALDNER
"Hammersley" porcelain, Thomas Goode and Co., London.

16 THE COMTESSE JEAN D'ORMESSON
Paper tablecloth, napkins, and plates, Lotus-Beghin-Say.

24 FRANÇOIS CATROUX
Tablemats and napkins, Manuel Canovas / glasses, copies of eighteenth-century pieces, Christian Dior.

28 JEAN SCHLUMBERGER
Jean Schlumberger cases, Tiffany's, New York.

30 HENRY CLARKE
Henry Clarke's book, *The Elegance of the Fifties,* is published by Herscher.

32 THE DUC AND DUCHESSE DE MOUCHY
Tablecloths, Simrane / glasses, Baccarat.

36 MADAME JEAN-LOUIS DUMAS
Plates, Le Toucan / tumblers, Hermès / chintz tablecloth, Manuel Canovas / picnic hamper, Keller from the Hermès Museum.

38 ANNE-MARIE DE GANAY
Hand-painted plates, trompe l'oeil cabbage, and glasses, Juste Mauve.

40 MONSIEUR AND MADAME GÉRALD VAN DER KEMP
Claude Monet's table service, Haviland et Parlon / glasses, Biot.

46 CLAUDE AND FRANÇOIS-XAVIER LALANNE
Carafe, François-Xavier Lalanne for Daum.

58 ISABELLE D'ORNANO
Eau de Campagne perfume, Sisley.

*Pénélope is an organization that helps people who make embroidered linen at home produce and sell it.

64 PRIMROSE BORDIER

Plates, Primose Bordier for Boyer / glasses, Primrose Bordier for
Les Cristalleries de Sèvres / paper napkins, Lotus-Beghin-Say /
baguettes, CFOC.

66 ALAIN-DOMINIQUE PERRIN

Plates, House of Cartier, Bernardaud / glasses, Cartier,
Compagnie Française du Cristal / silverware, Cartier, Reed &
Barton, U.S.A. / pad, metal cup, pen, and lighter, Cartier /
embroidered mats, Pénélope.

68 ANDRÉE PUTMAN

Cutlery, Andrée Putman for Siècle / porcelain, Andrée Putman
for Della Torre.

78 THE DUCHESSE DE SABRAN-PONTEVÈS

Tea set, Thomas Goode and Co., London / Apt faience plates,
Atelier Jean Faucon. The book by the Duchesse de Sabran- Pontevès,
Bon sang ne peut mentir, is published by Éditions J.-C Lattès.

82 BRUNO ROY

Mask, Alberto Valese, Venice.

84 KARL LAGERFELD

Etched crystal glasses, Val Saint-Lambert.

88 THE MARQUISE DE BRISSAC

Cups, Villeroy & Boch / cut glass, Waterford.

94 GUY DE ROUGEMONT

Cotton cloth, Boussac / plates, Artcurial / Diderot armchair and
chairs inlaid with six types of wood, triple stamped Rougemont,
Briard (cabinet-maker), and Artcurial.

96 CHRISTIAN LACROIX

Furniture, Garouste and Bonetti, Galerie Neotu.

98 CATHERINE OF RUSSIA

Tablecloth, Pénélope / plates, Mottahedeh / eighteenth-century
etched Bohemian crystal from Philippe Leroux / metalwork,
Puiforcat / chair, Bernard Steinitz.

102 COCO CHANEL

Etched glasses, Guillaume Saalburg / tablecloth, Pénélope /
clothes, accessories, and plates lent courtesy of Maison Chanel.

104 ATALANTA DE CASTELLANE

Plates, Haviland et Parlon / metalwork, Puiforcat / "Prestige"
glasses, Baccarat / carpet, Mikaeloff.

106 *MADAMA BUTTERFLY*

Porcelain, Lafarge / crystal, Saint-Louis / metalwork, Puiforcat / tablecloth, Pénélope.

108 EUGÈNE DE BEAUHARNAIS
Porcelain, Edward Memory for Puiforcat / crystal, Saint-Louis /
metalwork, Odiot / tablecloth and coverlet, Pénélope; design,
Pierre-Hervé Walbaum / replica of Biennais lamp, Odiot.

112 JEAN PUIFORCAT
Trouville silver cutlery, 1937; porcelain, 1935, Jean Puiforcat /
"Argos" glasses, Lalique / tablemats, Pénélope / flower
arrangement, Ninin Barrus.

120 MANUEL CANOVAS
Moiré tablecloth, Manuel Canovas / napkins, Porthault / cutlery,
Peter / glasses, Baccarat / "Galuchat" plates, Manuel Canovas for
Puiforcat / wine carafe, Lalique / the Niderwiller *rafraîchissoirs*
were made for the Würtemberg family.

124 LESLEY BLANCH-GARY
Lesley Blanch-Gary's book, *Pierre Loti,* is published by Seghers.

130 JEAN DIVE
"Micheletis" plates, Saint-Martin-de-Cros / cutlery, Scof.

132 WALTER LEES
Steel and plastic cutlery, Scof / vermeil coffeepot, Garrard.

144 KENZO
Haiku, Gonsui / The dish—turnip with prawns and broccoli—
is a creation by Kenzo's friend, chef Issé Soudo.

148 LAURA AND CORINNE MENTZELOPOULOS
"Matignon" porcelain and "Seville" dessert plates, Haviland et
Parlon / cheese plates, copies of "Châteaux" service, Deshoulières
/ "Symphony" metalwork, Odiot / glasses, Baccarat.

182 MICHAEL PRENTICE
Table in black South African granite, Michael Prentice for SAD, 1985.

192 THE PRIME MINISTER AND MADAME JACQUES
CHIRAC
"Perfection" glasses, Baccarat / "Matignon" breakfast plates,
Haviland et Parlon.

196 MADAME DIDIER WIRTH
Moustiers faience, Atelier de Segriès / Blue glasses, Nason
Moretti.

206 JACQUELINE HAGNAUER
Cashmere tablecloth, Martine Nourissat.

210 THE BARON DE CONDÉ
Alain de Condé exhibits in Paris at the galerie Bruno Ract-
Madoux.